99 Ways to Build Job Security

99 Ways to Build Job Security

Gary Nowinski

WATERBROOK
PRESS

99 WAYS TO BUILD JOB SECURITY
PUBLISHED BY WATERBROOK PRESS
12265 Oracle Boulevard, Suite 200
Colorado Springs, Colorado 80921

Scripture epigraphs for chapters 1, 3, 4, 6, and 7 are from The Message by Eugene H. Peterson. Copyright © 1993, 1994, 1995, 1996, 2000, 2001, 2002. Used by permission of NavPress Publishing Group. All rights reserved. Scripture epigraph for chapter 2 is from the New Century Version®. Copyright © 1987, 1988, 1991 by Thomas Nelson Inc. Used by permission. All rights reserved. Scripture epigraph for chapter 5 is taken from the Holy Bible, New International Version®. NIV®. Copyright © 1973, 1978, 1984 by International Bible Society. Used by permission of Zondervan Publishing House. All rights reserved.

ISBN 978-0-307-45840-7
ISBN 978-0-307-45846-9 (electronic)

Published in the United States by WaterBrook Multnomah, an imprint of the Crown Publishing Group, a division of Random House Inc., New York.

WATERBROOK and its deer colophon are registered trademarks of Random House Inc.

Library of Congress Cataloging-in-Publication Data
Nowinski, Gary.
    99 ways to build job security / Gary Nowinski.—1st ed.
        p. cm.
    ISBN 978-0-307-45840-7—ISBN 978-0-307-45846-9 (electronic) 1. Job security.
2. Employee motivation. 3. Employees—Attitude. 4. Performance. I. Title. II. Title:
Ninety nine ways to build job security.
    HD5708.4.N69 2009
    650.14—dc22

                                        2009009311

Printed in the United States of America
2009—First Edition

10 9 8 7 6 5 4 3 2 1

SPECIAL SALES
Most WaterBrook Multnomah books are available at special quantity discounts when purchased in bulk by corporations, organizations, and special-interest groups. Custom imprinting or excerpting can also be done to fit special needs. For information, please e-mail SpecialMarkets@WaterBrookMultnomah.com or call 1-800-603-7051.

Contents

Introduction

In tough economic times, maintaining your job security can be a dicey affair. Employers are constantly looking for ways to save money. Cutting staff is sometimes the first option, but often the last. No matter when it happens, it still hurts.

When employers are faced with reducing their staff, they evaluate each employee. They look at work history, attitude, accomplishments, and other factors to decide who stays and who goes. Some layoffs are determined by how long a person has been on the job, but there are times when longevity isn't the deciding factor.

More and more companies are taking quality and attitude into consideration. If they have a choice between an experienced employee with poor communication skills and less-than-desirable personal qualities and a less experienced person who is confident, trustworthy, and maintains a professional attitude, who do you think will be kept on the team? The more professional one will stay while the other hits the sidewalk.

This book contains ninety-nine practical things you can do

to help build your job security. Some are fairly easy to implement while others will take a lot of soul searching and a commitment to change. Some of the suggestions are steps you can take right now, but there are other tips that will require an investment of time or money or both.

Some factors that affect job security are completely out of your hands, such as when a company goes bankrupt and closes. You can't do much about that except pray, which is always a good idea because God cares deeply about what happens in your life. But you do have control over how you use the suggestions in this book. If you will put into practice the advice in just one of these chapters, it will affect in a significant way how your superiors value your employment.

1 Behavior and Attitude

The diligent find freedom in their work;
the lazy are oppressed by work.
—PROVERBS 12:24

Whether you realize it or not, your attitude and how you behave on the job are noticed daily. Consciously or subconsciously, your superiors are taking note of your attitude and watching how you interact with other employees, supervisors, and customers.

How you come across to your boss could be the difference between keeping and losing your job if pink slips are on the horizon. So it's important to be aware of how your behavior in the workplace is perceived.

It doesn't matter if you work in an office for a Fortune 500 company or on the line at a factory, the suggestions contained in this chapter will help you develop and maintain the kinds of behaviors that make a great impression on your colleagues and superiors alike.

1 LOYALTY

Loyalty in an employee is something that *all* employers seek. Years ago companies didn't have to worry so much about worker loyalty—people would stay with the same company for years, even decades. Today, however, nearly 65 percent of workers stay with an organization less than five years.

Employers crave loyalty, so you need to do all you can to demonstrate you are a truly loyal employee. You can do this with a few simple actions:

- *Research.* Find out all you can about the business and its leadership.
- *Go the extra mile.* Ask what you can do to help the organization.
- *Volunteer.* If the company plans a special activity or celebration, volunteer to help in its organization or implementation or both.
- *Don't broadcast job searches.* Even if you are looking for another job elsewhere, don't let a co-worker know—word will eventually get to the boss.

2 HONESTY/TRUSTWORTHINESS

Nothing appeals more to an employer than an honest employee. Employing someone who is truthful, reliable, and trustworthy is a business asset of immeasurable value. If your superiors know they can depend on you to always be honest and truthful, then you have a distinct advantage over others when it comes to job security.

An honest employee is one who doesn't steal time by coming in a few minutes late or taking an extended lunch simply because there's no time clock to punch. A trustworthy employee is one who doesn't engage in workplace thievery—taking pens, pencils, sticky notes, tools, and other company-owned items home for personal use.

Honesty also extends to your résumé. More and more companies engage third parties to check the validity of information on your résumé. One lie on your résumé can negate other valuable experience. So play it safe. Being truthful pays many more dividends than dishonesty.

3 INTEGRITY

Integrity goes hand in hand with honesty and trustworthiness. In the workplace, a person of integrity is known throughout the organization as someone who is always truthful, honest, straightforward, and reliable. A reputation of integrity will set you apart from others and keep you in good standing with your superiors.

But how do you establish a reputation as a person of integrity? Here are a few suggestions:

- Do what you say you're going to do.
- Be ethical—do the right thing—in all your business dealings.
- Be honest in your communication with colleagues and customers.
- Don't pass the blame for mistakes. Accept responsibility for your actions.
- Avoid hypocrisy and favoritism.

The Golden Rule is always a great place to start for building integrity in the workplace—treat others as you would like to be treated. And finally, act in private as you would if the whole world were watching.

4 EMPATHY

In today's economy, with layoffs and downsizing decimating workplace relationships, empathy is needed more than ever before.

In short, a person with empathy is someone who can identify with and understand another's situation, feelings, or motives. In the workplace, the ability to empathize with customers, colleagues, and superiors will increase your value as an employee.

Wherever you work, how you interact with the people around you gets noticed. Empathy allows you to better connect with those you come in contact with and helps establish a closer relationship.

So take some time and think of how you could show more empathy at work. Try being more sensitive to the people you interact with. Offer to help if a person is struggling. Sometimes, demonstrating empathy is as simple as listening when a person needs to talk. A nonjudgmental listener is a truly valuable asset.

5 LIKABILITY

You may be a great worker. You know your job and you get things done. But if people don't like you, it could make the difference between keeping your job and heading to the unemployment office. It may not be fair, but it's life—employers keep and promote the people they like.

Increasing your likability at work doesn't take a lot of effort. Here are a few simple things you can do to make yourself a more likable person:

- *Treat people with respect.* Respect is essential if you want people to like you.
- *Friendliness.* This can be shown as easily as saying "Good morning" or asking a colleague about his family. When a new employee joins the company, be the first to greet her.

- *Show concern.* Demonstrate empathy and relate to a co-worker who may be having a difficult time, offering help when you can.

6 SELF-CONFIDENCE

If you want to stand out in the crowd, a little self-confidence goes a long way.

Self-confidence is a certainty and trust in yourself that you have the skills and knowledge to accomplish a given task. It is an essential tool for effective performance and gives your superiors the reassurance they need to value you as an employee. Conversely, if you struggle with low self-confidence, your colleagues will notice and have doubts about your abilities, making your position more tenuous.

If you struggle with self-confidence, the following suggestions should help:

- First, try setting realistic goals for yourself. Don't set the bar too high initially. Establish an objective that you know you can reach. The more you hit your targets, the more your confidence grows.
- Don't get bogged down by past failures and negative self-talk. Learn from your mistakes and fill your mind with positive thoughts.

7 RISK TAKING

Risk taking in the workplace can be…well…risky. On the one hand, you have established methods and procedures that superiors take very seriously. Stray just a little and it could mean trouble. But taking risks with an eye toward innovation can be the key to more secure employment.

With rapidly changing technology and economic challenges, the ability to adapt and offer new and innovative ideas will not only demonstrate your company loyalty, but it will show your superiors that you have initiative—another highly desirable quality in employees.

But before strapping on the bungee cord and jumping off headfirst, it's best to gain a good understanding of what your company would consider an acceptable risk. Some managers really frown on failure, which is always possible when taking risks. Test the waters by talking to your superiors. If they seem receptive to subtle hints about risks, take your shot.

8 PRIDE

Taking pride in your job, your accomplishments, and your company is one of the more visible ways you can demonstrate your value to the ones who control your job security.

When you take pride in the work you do, it shows in your demeanor, in the quality of your work, and in compliments from colleagues and customers. People can tell if you are proud of your work or just going through the motions. So no matter if you're flipping burgers or designing rockets, do it to the best of your ability and take pride in what you've accomplished. Others will notice.

Pride in the company you work for is another highly visible way to endear yourself to your superiors. So when appropriate, wear clothing bearing the company logo, volunteer at company-sponsored events, and don't be afraid to brag about your employer.

9 FLEXIBILITY

No, most employers are not looking for people who can do the splits or easily sit in the lotus position! However, someone who can roll with the punches and not be fazed by change is a person of great value.

Flexibility is an important trait for any employee. No matter the industry or job, rarely can you go through a week or even a day with everything staying completely the same. Change happens. The person who can adapt to change and do it *without complaining or showing frustration* is the one who gets noticed.

When you demonstrate adaptability, it shows your superiors that you value the organization and will do what it takes to see that its mission succeeds.

So when change comes—and it will—embrace it. And no matter how many twists and turns take place, display a positive, can-do attitude.

 **TENACITY**

Employers aren't looking for quitters who give up at the first sign of trouble. They value employees who are tenacious, people who will get the job done no matter what.

Tenacity can make the difference between success and failure. If you persevere in the face of adversity, if you keep going no matter what obstacles come your way, if your superiors know that they can count on you to do whatever it takes to finish a project, then you've got a huge advantage over others when layoffs are imminent.

Tenacity pays off in other areas. When presenting new ideas, don't give up at the first rejection. The old adage is true: "If at first you don't succeed, try, try again." Naturally, be aware of how hard to push; some managers bristle when you're overbearing. But don't be afraid to stand up for your ideas. Persistence often pays off.

11 Manners Matter

Practicing proper manners is always a good idea, but it's especially important in the workplace.

It often seems like pleasant manners went out with the typewriter. People get caught up in the cares of life and simply forget to treat others with courtesy and respect. But with manners sorely lacking in the workplace, when someone uses them consistently, it gets noticed.

The fact is, people like people who use appropriate manners. It shows that you care for the people around you and demonstrates first-rate teamwork.

Practicing good manners in the workplace isn't really that hard. Just try these simple suggestions:

- Always say please and thank you.
- Open doors for people.
- Use proper telephone and cell phone etiquette.
- Don't be late for meetings.
- Avoid crude or crass communication. Maintain a professional tone in e-mail.

Using appropriate manners could mean the difference between saving and losing your job or a promotion.

12 ATTENDANCE

Nothing screams louder, "I couldn't care less about this job," than poor attendance.

Attendance is one of the biggest issues employers take into account when evaluating whether to keep or release an employee. It's also the easiest to track. Realize it or not, your boss knows your attendance habits.

For salaried employees especially, the temptation to cheat a few minutes here and there can cause real problems. With no time clock to punch, who's to know if you come in at 8 a.m. or 8:05? Tardiness equals poor evaluations. So keep an eye on your tardiness; your boss certainly does.

And watch your sick days. Most people are not sick enough throughout the year to legitimately use all their sick days. Using all your sick days is often a sign of employee dissatisfaction and could put you at the top of the RIF (reduction in force) list.

13 WORKPLACE POLITICS

Like it or not, workplace politics is a fact of life. Now, I'm not talking about red or blue states or donkeys and elephants here. I mean the kind of politics that can affect your standing within an organization or how you're treated by others. It thrives in nearly every office within almost every organization.

Office politics can be a source of great tension, stress, and anxiety. Sometimes it's like experiencing high school all over again, where cliques and favoritism abound. And it's often a new employee who experiences the most discrimination. Although many organizations try to limit this kind of on-the-job politicking, it still happens.

So learn as quickly as you can how your workplace operates and the political hierarchy. And if you find yourself the victim of office politics, there are two time-tested ways to overcome it: kill them with kindness and turn the other cheek.

14 MAINTAIN FOCUS

Distractions are a way of life and hard to avoid in the workplace. Employees who are able to maintain their focus and complete a job are a valuable resource for employers.

Maintaining focus helps you to be more productive and do higher-quality work. To help you sustain your focus, try these simple tips:

- *Eliminate distractions.* Clear your work area, shut off the iPod or radio, ignore e-mail for at least short periods, arrange everything you need to complete your task, and mute your phone.

- *Leave visual reminders in easy sight.* Some of us need visual cues to help us stay on task. Strategically placed sticky notes can really help.
- *Set easy-to-reach deadlines.* Sometimes, when you look at a project in its entirety, getting to the end can seem pretty intimidating. Setting easy-to-reach deadlines can make the task more manageable.
- *Take short, frequent breaks.* Stepping away momentarily does wonders for focus.

15 ⟩ KEEP A POSITIVE ATTITUDE

If you really want to stand out in your boss's mind and leave a good impression with your colleagues, the best way to do it is to maintain a positive attitude.

People are naturally drawn to those who are always positive. A person with a positive attitude exudes confidence. With so many things that can go wrong in the workplace, interacting with a positive person can give you the self-assurance to persevere.

Your attitude makes all the difference in how your day goes and how others perceive your value as an employee. If you complain all the time and radiate pessimism, what makes you think that you'll be the person who survives the next round of layoffs?

So no matter what's going on around you, be a beacon of encouragement and positive thoughts to your co-workers. You'll soon discover how valuable an employee you really are.

SUMMARY

Your attitude and how you behave on the job are key aspects of how you are perceived as an employee. If your superiors see you as someone with a poor attitude or with negative behaviors, what are your chances of surviving a layoff? You may be a good worker, but if your attitude stinks, you're gone.

Employers value people who are

- positive, honest, loyal, flexible, and known for integrity;
- risk takers, tenacious, filled with self-confidence, and proud of the work they do and the company they serve.

If you are an employee who is focused and well mannered, who goes the extra mile to get the job done, you can feel much more secure in your employment. If not, your job security may be in jeopardy.

2 Education and Training

Happy is the person who finds wisdom,
the one who gets understanding.

—Proverbs 3:13

If you want to take job security into your own hands, your best bet is to get educated. Learning new and valuable skills will not only increase your self-confidence and feelings of worth, it will also increase your value as an employee.

Even after years of schooling, internships, and training, doctors and nurses participate in several hours of continuing education every year, as do teachers and other business professionals. You should do nothing less.

Motivation is a key component to education. With that in mind, answer this question: how strong is your motivation to keep your job?

No matter what your occupation or level of experience, improving, updating, or learning new skills will make you a more valuable asset to your employer.

16 IMPROVE CURRENT SKILLS

You are probably very skilled at your job. But it doesn't matter how experienced you are; there's always room for improvement. The better and more finely tuned your abilities, the more you will stand out to your superiors.

With technology growing exponentially these days, it's hard to be completely up to date with everything. The only way to stay ahead of the curve is to embrace new and emerging technologies and learn how to use them to work for you and benefit your company.

If you work in construction, learn as much as you can about the industry. If you work in an office, improve your communication and keyboarding skills. If you work in a fast-food establishment, try studying restaurant management.

There are many free resources available online and in libraries, thus keeping the cost of improving your abilities within easy financial reach. Remember, improving your skills *will* make you a more valuable employee.

17 LEARN NEW SKILLS

Regardless of your profession, learning new skills can be an interesting and exciting way to increase your value within the workplace. A well-rounded employee is a true asset to a company. The more skills you have, the more attractive you are to an employer.

In an era where more and more organizations are tightening their belts, the person with talent and skills will still be around when others are cleaning out their desks. So it's important to set yourself apart by acquiring new abilities.

Here are a few ideas for discovering what to study:

- Research the skills your employer feels are required to do your job.
- Research what other professionals in your field consider as required skills.
- Ask your human resources person for a copy of your job description.
- Keep an eye on internal job postings.
- For better customer communication, learn a foreign language.

18 ANTICIPATE NEEDS AND GET TRAINED

Initiative is an important asset for any organization. It gives you a golden opportunity to make a fabulous impression on your superiors. That's why you need to take the initiative by anticipating the future needs of the company you work for and get trained to meet those needs.

Research is key to anticipating the future needs of an organization. Keeping up on industrial trends, researching emerging technologies, and reading periodicals pertinent to your business are all great ways to discover what the future holds.

Once your research is done, find out where and how you can get trained to accomplish the task and fill a void when the need arises. This will not only show great initiative but will put you in good standing with your superiors, thus improving your job security.

19 SOFTWARE TRAINING

If you work in an office of any type, your computer-software knowledge could mean the difference between a job with a firm foundation or one that's on sinking sand. The more proficient you are in using programs common to your line of work, the greater your value as an employee.

Regardless if you use a PC or a Mac, the most common applications used across the country are included in Microsoft Office Suites. So knowing your way around Word, Excel, Power-Point, and Outlook is an essential part of most office-related work.

While most people have a basic knowledge of these applications, the more adept you are at using them, the more valuable you are to your employer. So learn all you can about using macros; inserting tables, graphs, and charts; and formatting spreadsheets. Be the go-to person when co-workers or managers need help on a PowerPoint presentation. You'll quickly prove your worth.

20 ⟩ Improve Keyboarding Speed

Knowing your way around computer applications is a valuable skill. But your proficiency with a keyboard is no less beneficial. The speedier you are at using a computer keyboard, the greater your worth as an employee.

There are several advantages to improving your keyboarding aptitude, such as greater productivity and spending less time staring at your monitor. Studies show that people who type with ten fingers make fewer mistakes and suffer less wrist pain.

Competent keyboarding also encompasses understanding ten-key, that is, using the number pad to the right of the keyboard for data entry.

There are several free Web sites where you can practice and hone your typing and ten-key skills. You may want to purchase or download one of the many keyboarding tutorials available online.

So spend some time improving your keyboarding skills. It will really pay off.

21 LEARN HOW TO OPERATE AND FIX OFFICE EQUIPMENT

Knowing how to operate office equipment may seem trivial when it comes to job security. However, if you have the ability to not only operate office equipment but also to teach others how to use the equipment and even get it working when it breaks down, then you have a distinct advantage over other employees.

With the right tools, a little research, and a modicum of mechanical ability, you can become an expert at fixing minor fax, copier, and printer problems. Here are a few simple tips:

- Keep some tweezers and a small flashlight at your desk: these are handy for removing stubborn, hard-to-see paper jams.
- Don't be afraid to touch the copy-machine toner: if you get it on your hands, it washes right off.
- Clean glass equals clean copies: make sure the glass on your copier is clean or you'll have poor copies.
- Read operating manuals.

22 ⟩ GET YOUR DIPLOMA/GED

Nothing opens more doors than having your diploma. It's the key to every opportunity.

Sure, there are some very successful people who never graduated from high school, but their numbers are minuscule. Nearly all employers out there, including the military, require at least a GED before they bring you on. Employers need to know that you have the intelligence to perform. A diploma is their first clue that you do.

It's never too late to get your diploma. A recent news article told the story of a high school graduate who was almost one hundred years old. Nearly every school district in the nation has some kind of program to help you graduate. And there are plenty of ways to get your diploma online, from the comfort of your home.

If you're not inclined to attend school, at least get your GED. It opens the doors to higher education and far greater opportunities.

23 ⟩ RESEARCH ADULT EDUCATION OPTIONS

The thought of going back to school may be intimidating to some people, especially if you've been out for several years. But there are several options available to adults these days. Your task is to find the one that best suits you and your other obligations.

The great thing about adult education is that the instructors understand the special needs and abilities we have. Classes are often geared toward the needs of the students, not the teachers. Most classes are held in the evening, so people can attend after work.

There are several colleges and universities that offer accelerated learning. These are courses where you attend one or two nights a week for up to four hours. But each course lasts only a few weeks, allowing you to complete a four-year degree in only two years.

Research your options and hit the books; it'll pay great dividends.

24 ⟩ COMMUNITY COLLEGE

Community colleges are a great resource for updating, improving, or learning new skills. They're also an excellent place to start if you're heading back to school to seek an undergraduate degree.

Most larger cities have at least one community college. They offer occupational training and programs to help you obtain an associate's degree. Most offer day and evening classes to accommodate working people's schedules. Several even offer online courses.

At a community college, you can learn computer applications, carpentry, effective communication skills, and just about any skill you need to improve your value in the workplace. And the plus is that they are usually much less expensive than colleges of the four-year variety.

So if you've been out of school awhile, start at a community college rather than a four-year university—it'll help you get back into learning mode without the added cost.

 ## 25 NIGHT SCHOOL

Since most people work during the day, night school is a great way to obtain your high school or college diploma, learn new skills or improve current ones, or learn an entirely new occupation.

Evening classes are generally geared toward adults, although it's not uncommon to find younger people sitting alongside you. Because instructors are dealing with a more mature audience—people who actually *want* to be in school—lessons are often more focused, which creates a better atmosphere for learning.

One thing to remember about attending school in the

evening, especially after a full workday, is that you sometimes need to make a rigorous effort to stay alert during lectures.

And take this from personal experience: if you can, don't take a class on a Friday evening. There's something about sitting in school on a Friday night that is psychologically demanding. And besides that, it just seems wrong!

26 CORRESPONDENCE COURSES

Correspondence courses are a great way to get the education and training you need at your own pace, from the comfort of your own home. They are an excellent option for single moms, people who live in rural settings, and those who may cringe at the thought of stepping into an educational institution.

These days you can find correspondence courses covering just about any topic you can think of, but the ones dealing with professional development are the most valuable.

But do your research. There are some disreputable organizations out there that will take your money and give you nothing in return.

One way to ensure you're not going to be scammed is to look for courses offered by accredited schools or universities. The advantage of this is that when you're done, you'll have credits that will count toward a college degree.

27 ONLINE EDUCATION

The great thing about today's technology is that it can bring higher education right into your home. Over the last ten years, online education has exploded. Nearly every university in the country offers online degree programs, even Ivy League schools.

Of course, you need to have a computer with Internet access; a broadband or other high-speed connection is also very helpful, as are external speakers. Word-processing software is vital.

Just as in a traditional classroom, you will have instructors for all your online courses. They often have video lectures posted for you to view. Much of your communication with the instructor takes place through e-mail.

If you're not interested in obtaining college credits and just want to learn skills helpful to your job, there are several Web sites where you can find the training you need at a fraction of the cost of an accredited institution.

28 FREE EDUCATION AND TRAINING

In a tough economy, we're all looking for ways to save money. However, training to update or improve your skills can be cost prohibitive. That's when you need to research options for free or very low-cost training.

The Internet is loaded with free education and training sites. Whether you want software training, information on how to improve your customer service skills, or if you want to learn how to make English toffee, it's all there waiting for you online.

You do have to be aware, however, that when it comes to free education, many times you get what you pay for. But there are some very good training sites where you can receive information that will help you gain the knowledge you need to make a difference.

Another place to find free training, which is often overlooked, is YouTube.com. There you'll find informative training videos on several different, very useful subjects.

SUMMARY

If you want to make a good impression on your superiors, you need to take time to obtain the knowledge and skills required to not only do your job but to excel at it. That takes training.

This chapter has given you several methods and reasons for educating yourself. But the choice is yours. You're the one who needs to get the training; nobody is going to do it for you. You can cruise along with the skills you currently have, but if you want to soar above the others and increase your value as an employee, then research your education options and hit the books.

You may not only keep your job, you'll make yourself more promotable. Wouldn't that be nice?

3 Communication

The one who knows much says little;
an understanding person remains calm.
—PROVERBS 17:27

Effective communication in the workplace is vital to an organization's and an employee's success. If you have the ability to communicate well, it can open the doors to greater opportunities and increase your value.

Being able to communicate effectively is more than just speaking well. It is the ability to correspond in such a way that you know your intentions are understood and that you clearly understand others. But be aware, we also communicate in ways that are not verbal but speak very loudly.

We've probably all been in situations where a lack of communication caused anger, frustration, hurt feelings, and time delays. The better you are at avoiding these situations in the workplace, the more productive and happier you will be.

29   YOUR WORK IS A PERPETUAL JOB INTERVIEW

Wherever you work and whatever your profession, the people you work for and with are judging you daily. Does the way you come across to your superiors make them think that you like your job or that you're simply going through the motions? What kind of image do you portray? If you're unsure, try thinking of your job as a perpetual job interview.

When you go to an interview, you always put your best foot forward. You look sharp, you're clean, you're enthusiastic, and you portray an image of confidence and sincere interest in the position and the company. If you want to impress your superiors, try approaching your job like that every day.

The image you communicated during your interview caused your superiors to select you over all the other applicants. So treat every day like an interview. The results will be worth the effort.

30   COMMUNICATE CLEARLY

Have you ever been in a meeting where you left having no idea what it was all about? We hear messages every day, but not many of them actually stick. One of the reasons for this is that we're not being communicated to in a clear manner. If you take the time to always communicate clearly, your stock will rise within your organization.

Try these suggestions to help improve the clarity of your message:

- *Use a personal touch.* With the dawn of the Internet came e-mail. E-mail is a wonderful tool, but it can cause problems with communication too. Whenever possible, get up from your desk, take a short walk, and talk with a person face to face. Clear communication is much easier in person.

- *Don't be afraid to ask questions.* There is nothing wrong with saying, "I don't understand" or "Would you repeat that?" True understanding leads to clear communication.

31 VERBAL COMMUNICATION

Verbal communication involves the words that come out of our mouths. But it's more than just words—it's also how you say things. It's volume, inflection, articulation, tone, even attitude. If you are a person who excels at verbal communication, then you have an advantage over others who do not.

Clarity is key for effective verbal communication. So before you head off to your meeting or make an important phone call, be sure to have all your points outlined and organized. This will help you speak with clarity and confidence.

A person with good verbal communication skills doesn't mumble or speak too softly. People need to be able to understand what you are saying, and they need to be able to hear it. So be bold, speak up, and be sure to enunciate.

Also be careful of the words you use. Using crass or inappropriate words severely muddles your message.

32 ACTIVE LISTENING

One of the most important aspects of effective communication is the art of active listening.

When you're interacting with someone at work or in your personal life, does your mind tend to wander when the other person is speaking? Are you distracted by things around you or thinking of how you will respond to what is being said? If so, then you are not engaged in active listening.

Active listening takes effort. It involves paying attention to what is being said and responding in a way that focuses attention on the speaker. Active listening helps both parties in a discussion to be fully engaged and to fully understand what is being said, thereby minimizing miscommunication.

Here are a few ideas to help:

- Take brief notes.
- Pay attention.
- Eliminate interruptions.
- Provide feedback.
- Paraphrase what is being said.
- Ask open-ended questions.
- Practice empathy by putting yourself in the other person's shoes.

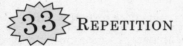 REPETITION

Repetition can be a useful tool in the quest for effective communication. It's also one of the easiest to use. Repetition is simply repeating what you have said or asking someone to repeat what she has said. See, that's pretty easy.

We get into trouble when we assume that everything we say is understood completely. But more often than not, points are missed. Repetition works because each person involved in a conversation knows exactly what is being said. If a remark is not understood, simply asking the comment to be repeated brings clarity.

Repetition is vital when setting appointments or when numbers are involved. I'm sure we've all had times when we've given someone a phone number or address only to have him go to the wrong house or call the wrong number. Mistakes also happen when setting appointment times and dates. Repeating information eliminates mistakes and brings better communication.

34 PARAPHRASING

Another effective communication tool that goes along with active listening and repetition is paraphrasing. This is where you use your own words to repeat a comment back to a speaker. Paraphrasing is another great way to eliminate miscommunication.

Paraphrasing gives you the ability to form a connection with a colleague by demonstrating that you care about what she is saying—that you are truly interested in understanding her position or message. It takes some getting used to, but once you master the art of paraphrasing, your communication skills will soar.

Paraphrasing usually starts with a comment such as "So what you're saying is…" or "Okay, let me see if I understand you correctly." These simple phrases followed by your explanation of what you heard communicated will do wonders to bring clarity and understanding. You'll also have the added benefit of making your bosses and colleagues feel valued and respected.

 Follow Up

Okay, you're well on your way to improving your communication skills. You're engaging in active listening, you're using repetition and paraphrasing, and you're focusing on communicating clearly. Is there anything else you can do to ensure effective communication? Yes indeed—follow up.

Even if you've done everything right, sometimes people misunderstand or miss things. That's where following up on a conversation is very beneficial. Following up is simply making contact after a meeting or discussion to ensure that everybody is still on the same page. It's especially useful if there are several people in an office who need to hear the message. You never know who may have missed it.

So follow up by sending e-mails, letters, or faxes; make phone calls; write memos; send a text message; whatever you feel is the most effective way to ensure that there is no miscommunication or misunderstanding. It will save embarrassment and demonstrate your initiative.

36 Eliminate Bad Listening Habits

As much as good listening habits and communication skills can enhance your career, bad listening habits can put it in peril.

Bad listening habits include:

- Thinking of responses: when you're thinking of how to respond, you obviously aren't concentrating on what's being said.
- Finishing another person's sentences: this demonstrates impatience and is quite annoying.
- Interrupting: a very irritating habit; interrupting also shows disrespect.
- A wandering mind: when you allow your mind to wander, you inadvertently miss key points of a conversation.

The key to effective communication is to recognize your shortcomings in the area of listening and take steps to change.

If you have any of the habits listed above, it's important for you to discipline yourself and concentrate. Focus in on the speaker and what's being said. Take brief notes. And if you interrupt and finish sentences a lot, give others permission to stop you.

37 BIASED AND DEFENSIVE LISTENING

Two more bad listening habits that are essential to identify and eliminate are biased listening and defensive listening. These are two of the most insidious barriers to good communication.

When you go into a conversation with personal bias toward the person you are speaking with, the success of your discussion is at risk from the start. People have all kinds of biases toward others, because of a past slight, race, age, gender, geographical upbringing, or any number of other reasons.

Defensive listening is where you have a tendency to take anything said as a personal attack. Your defenses immediately go up, and no matter what's being said, clear communication goes up in smoke.

It's important for you to identify these bad listening habits before going into a conversation, especially when a conflict is involved. When you are aware of your listening problems, you can more easily put them aside.

38 NONVERBAL COMMUNICATION

Nonverbal communication, not what is said with words or phrases, but what your body and attitude say, is actually more important than the words you use. Over 50 percent of communication is nonverbal. So knowledge of how we communicate without words is a valuable skill in the workplace.

Many people equate nonverbal communication with just body language. But there's a lot more to it than that. It involves dress, grooming, facial expressions, posture, manners, and any number of other factors.

The two sayings "Actions speak louder than words" and "A picture is worth a thousand words" are all too true when it comes to effective communication. For better or worse, how you act and look tells people how to respond to your message before you even start speaking.

What image do you want to portray? Figure that out and change your nonverbal communication accordingly.

39 BODY LANGUAGE

When you enter a room, do you project an image of confidence and self-assurance or one of insecurity or bored disinterest? What you do with your body speaks a hundred decibels louder than the words you use.

Body language is your first impression. Before a person hears the first word out of your mouth, she has already developed an opinion of you. Your body language may not be conveying how you really feel or think, so you need to be aware of what your body communicates.

Body Language Red Flags:
- Hands in your pockets suggests insecurity
- Arms crossed over chest is viewed as defensive
- Hands on hips indicates defiance

- Clenched fists communicates anxiety or tension
- Leaning back in a chair implies disinterest

Effective Body Language:

- Good posture portrays an image of confidence
- Maintaining eye contact conveys interest and respect
- Using hand gestures demonstrates self-assurance

40 · FACIAL EXPRESSIONS

Simply put, facial expression is the way your face muscles respond to different situations. You may not be saying a word, but your face is speaking volumes. Be mindful of what your face is saying, or superiors could get the wrong impression.

Smiling, frowning, raising an eyebrow, scowling, smirking, even a lack of expression are all ways we use our face to convey a message. A smile usually communicates friendliness or agreement. A raised eyebrow conveys doubt or surprise. A frown expresses displeasure or anger. What is your face telling your colleagues?

Emotions play a big part in our facial expressions. The way our faces react to a situation is hard to control because our emotions cause an instinctive, spontaneous response. The key is to keep your emotions in check and to concentrate on maintaining an appropriate expression, one befitting the situation.

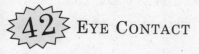

41 The Power of a Smile

At my local supermarket, there are two bag girls. One is your average bagging person—a pleasant, paper-or-plastic kind of personality. The other, Hannah, is always smiling and cheerful. When I check out, I usually try going to Hannah's station because my perception is that she is the better bagger.

There's nothing like a genuine smile to draw people in. It's like a magnet of positive feelings. It gives people the sense that you are confident, capable, and considerate. But be aware, people can usually spot a fake smile, which could cause them to think that you're less than sincere.

In customer service especially, if you can manage a genuine smile when working with customers, the more those customers are willing to help you help them. The power of a smile is one thing that keeps customers and clients coming back, something all bosses love.

42 Eye Contact

If there is one thing that gives the impression that you are interested and engaged in what someone is saying, it's eye contact. And if you want people to listen to you, maintain eye contact.

Making eye contact conveys interest and respect. On the

other hand, looking away or making very little eye contact leaves the impression that you are disinterested, nervous, or even arrogant.

So when you have interactions with your colleagues, superiors in particular, it's important that you give them the respect they deserve by sustaining eye contact. That can be easier said than done, however, so you may need to practice.

If you're not used to making eye contact, try practicing on your friends and family. Every time you speak with them, maintain eye contact for as long as you can. You'll find the more you do it, the easier it gets.

43 Ask Open-Ended Questions

Another valuable tool for effective communication is the practice of asking open-ended questions. These are the kinds of questions calling for more than a simple yes-or-no answer. The more information you gain from an answer, the better your communication.

Usually an open-ended question starts with words such as *Why* or *How* or *When,* not *Did* or *Are* or *Can.* But you can also use phrases such as "Explain why…" or "Tell me about…" While these phrases may not exactly be questions, they are statements that require a response.

Here are more examples of open-ended questions and statements:

- "What do you think about…?"
- "How do you think we could…?"
- "How else could we do that?"
- "Explain how you would…"
- "Tell me about why you…"
- "Detail what happened."

It takes practice, but the benefits of open-ended questions are quite valuable.

44 BARRIERS TO EFFECTIVE COMMUNICATION

No discussion of communication in the workplace is complete without touching on the barriers that diminish its effectiveness. Identifying and avoiding these barriers will allow you to communicate with confidence, giving you an advantage over your colleagues.

In any form of communication, there is a sender and a receiver. The job of the sender is to communicate the message so that the receiver understands it completely. But there are obstacles that can block all or parts of the message. They include:

- Gender
- Age

- Education
- Personality
- Personal bias

These barriers, or any of the many others you will encounter, can decimate your message, leading to miscommunication and misunderstanding. That's why it's important for you to pinpoint the barriers you encounter in the workplace and develop strategies for maneuvering your message through those obstacles successfully.

It's also a good idea to anticipate difficulties beforehand, leaving you better prepared.

SUMMARY

The employee with stellar communication skills is an asset to any organization. If you want to build job security, you need to increase your value as an employee. Improving your communication skills will do just that.

Here are the key points to remember:

- Think of your job as a perpetual job interview where you put your best foot forward every day.
- Practice good verbal and nonverbal communication, paying particular attention to communicating clearly, how you listen, your body language, and the image you project.
- Identify and clear away any roadblocks to communication.

Using the suggestions in this chapter will not only help improve your ability to communicate at work, but they also will help you in all aspects of your life.

4 Appearance and Grooming

Just as water mirrors your face,
so your face mirrors your heart.

—PROVERBS 27:19

Believe it or not, appearance and grooming do make a difference in how you are perceived by your superiors. It doesn't matter where you work or how casual the workplace, how you look is important.

Which construction worker looks like he cares more about his job, the one who arrives with a torn shirt, dirty jeans, and bed-head, or the one who looks clean, sharp, and well groomed? In an office, which customer service rep looks more professional, the one with a wrinkled blouse and flip-flops or the one with pressed clothes and pumps?

Image counts in the workplace, so you need to do all you can to stand out and look like the professional you are. The following suggestions will help you look your best.

⟨45⟩ The Whole Package

When you arrive at work for the day, your superiors are appraising more than just your qualifications; they're evaluating the whole package. Your attitude, the way you look, your posture, your demeanor, it all matters. You may have great qualifications, but if you seem to care less about your appearance, it could negate any positive feelings your superiors have about your experience.

So you need to take steps to project an image that will be appreciated by your boss and the people you work with, starting with how you dress. Does the way you dress convey an image of professionalism or incompetence? Do you abide by the company dress code or do you cheat a little here and there?

A good rule of thumb is to treat your appearance as if you were working with customers every day. You want to project an image of competence to your customers, right?

⟨46⟩ Look Professional

Looking like a professional is a head-to-toe endeavor. Employers want someone who looks like he knows what he's doing. The way you look can convey an attitude of confidence and pride or one of indifference. What does your boss feel when you walk in?

A professional look includes:

- *Hair.* Is it unkempt and dirty or clean and in place?
- *Neck and face.* Are they clean and shaved? Is makeup applied tastefully?
- *Clothes.* Do they fit? Are they clean and pressed?
- *Hands.* Are they clean? Are your fingernails dirty or too long?
- *Socks/Stockings.* Are they appropriate and free of holes?
- *Shoes.* Are they appropriate for your job and clean?

These are all things you need to consider when creating an appearance that looks professional, one that shows you care about your job and the people you work for and with.

47 CASUAL VS. SLOPPY

Casual days at work are great! You can leave the ties and pantyhose at home and wear comfortable clothes, maybe even sneakers! But just because the dress is casual, you need to be careful; there can be a fine line between casual and sloppy.

The rules for casual workdays can vary from one business to another. What's casual for one business may be totally inappropriate for another. Summertime casual dress can be particularly revealing, which can put you in a bad light.

The trick to casual day is to observe your superiors and

dress like them. Managers and executives will often dress the part, even on casual days. Very rarely will you see executives really dress down; they want to maintain a professional look. You should do the same.

So toss the printed T-shirts, forget the flip-flops, heave the halter top, and stow your shorts. Instead, dress for success.

 ## OFFICE BASICS

The way you dress makes a difference. It can have a significant impact on the way you are perceived as an employee. How you dress also reflects the values and professionalism of the organization you work for.

A good guide to dressing in a professional manner is to not get too flashy with the clothes you wear. Skip the highly colorful and patterned clothes and stay with something more basic. You want people to remember you, not what you are wearing.

For men, you want your closet to contain navy blue or dark gray suits, jackets, and pants. Women should stay away from clothes with too many frills like lace, ruffles, and other add-ons. A professional office look does not include plaids, stripes, or floral prints.

White shirts are also a plus because they go with everything and project a clean, professional image.

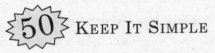 49 ⊰ Avoid the Artificial

Another characteristic of a professional office look is to avoid wearing clothes or designs that give an impression of artificiality. If people see you as artificial, they will be less trusting of you because you project an air of falseness. A more natural look projects an image of confidence and competence.

An artificial appearance is one where the clothes you wear make you look unnatural; for example, oversized shoulder pads, long artificial nails, sequins. An artificial look can also involve accessories and fabrics. So stay away from clothes made from man-made fabrics like acrylics and polyester. And get rid of plastic belts and accessories.

Your best bet is to stick with clothes and accessories made in natural colors from natural fabrics such as cotton, wool, silk, and leather. Shirts and blouses should be white, beige, or other natural colors. And leather shoes are a necessity for a natural, professional appearance.

50 ⊰ Keep It Simple

Being noticeable among your colleagues is important, but not if it's done through a gaudy appearance.

To make a good impression on your boss, use restraint in the way you dress and in your general appearance. Save personal expression for the weekend; make your work look simple and professional.

Here are a few suggestions for maintaining a simple, sharp, professional look:

- Keep your flashy suits and dresses in the closet.
- Limit your accessories and the amount of jewelry you wear.
- Suspenders are preferred over belts, but never wear both.
- Tone down makeup, especially around the eyes and in the amount of blush you use.

Today's cultural trends have brought multiple tattoos and piercings into the mainstream. But if you want to look professional, you'll keep all tattoos covered during business hours and pull the metal out of your face and tongue.

51 > MAKE SURE IT FITS

If there's anything that makes you look shabby, it's clothes that don't fit. We've all seen colleagues who arrive at work wearing dresses that are too small, slacks that are too tight, and shirts where the buttons are straining under the pressure. So it's important to wear clothes that fit.

When your clothes don't fit, you feel self-conscious; you're always checking yourself, tucking in your wayward shirttail, and making sure one of those buttons hasn't popped. All of this makes you feel less confident. But wearing clothes that fit gives you a more professional appearance and makes you feel more comfortable.

Signs that it's time to lose weight or buy larger clothes include:

- Shirts or blouses that gap across the chest
- Sleeves that pull above the wrist
- Pants or skirts with a pulled zipper
- Gaping pants pockets

Proper-fitting clothes are essential for a professional image.

52 ᐳ Make Sure It's Clean

This may seem like a no-brainer, but when you go to work, make sure your clothes are clean. Dirty or stained clothes scream, "I don't care what I look like or what you think of me."

Perhaps you've seen the TV ad with the talking stain. A guy is interviewing with a manager type, and everything he is saying is being drowned out by a mumbling stain on his shirt. This ad makes a great point: if you're trying to have an effective conversation with a colleague, your message gets drowned out by the loud stain on your shirt or blouse.

So take the time to check your wardrobe. Make sure what you wear to work is not only clean but stain free as well. It's also a good idea to make sure your clothes are properly pressed. Sharp pleats and starched collars demonstrate a truly professional image.

53 KEEP YOURSELF COVERED

Reputation means a lot in the workplace. If you arrive at work wearing clothes that show a lot of skin, instead of building a reputation as a professional, you are creating an image that you are unprofessional and probably foolish.

That's why it is so important to keep yourself covered if you want to maintain a professional persona. Men and women alike, here are things you need to do to keep yourself covered:

- Avoid plunging necklines.
- Trade low-rise pants and miniskirts in for more businesslike attire.
- Make sure no body hair is sneaking into view.
- Leave your shorts, see-through shirts, midriff-baring tops, tank tops, and open-back blouses at home.

In the summertime, the temptation is to wear a dress or top that may reveal more than you normally would. Don't take the bait. Keep yourself covered, and you'll show others that you truly care about your appearance, your reputation, and your job.

 54 STAY FIT

Like it or not, a big part of our appearance has to do with our weight. You may have all of the qualifications and experience in the world, but if you're overweight, your chances of landing and keeping a job are severely hampered.

When you're overweight, your health is at risk. Your superiors know this. If a reduction in force is planned, and your boss has to make a choice between a healthy person and one who is overweight or obese, which person is at greater risk? The one who may end up costing the company more in insurance premiums and lost time—the one with a weight problem, of course.

So if you value your job and your health, try to find ways to get fit. If your company has health facilities, use them. If reduced health-club rates are available, check into that. It's important to do something.

55 SHOES

Yeah, it may seem kind of silly, but shoes really do matter when it comes to your appearance and creating a professional look. You may be dressed and groomed quite well, but if you're wearing shoes that are worn or inappropriate, it will throw off your entire appearance.

When it comes to shoes for business, choose shoes in neutral colors that are in good condition and free of scuff marks. Flamboyant athletic shoes, slippers, flip-flops, thongs, and Doc Martens–type boots should be avoided, even on casual days.

Ladies, avoid the temptation to wear shoes with stiletto or unusually high heels. Open-toed shoes, sandals, shoes with ankle straps, and trendy styles should also be avoided. Instead, wear pumps with heels that aren't too high, ones in which you can walk in comfort.

Guys, your best bet for an office shoe is to pick something in a black wingtip or oxford.

56 GOOD GROOMING

No discussion of creating a professional appearance and how you are perceived by others is complete without discussing the importance of grooming. It's something your superiors notice and could make or break you when tough staffing decisions are made.

First impressions are vital to the way your superiors perceive you as an employee. You may wow them when you first start, but after a while, you begin to get comfortable and complacent about grooming. For example:

- You come in with dirty or unkempt hair.
- You haven't shaved for a few days.

- You emit an odor that exposes the fact that you haven't bathed in a day or two.
- Your hands are dry, nails untrimmed and dirty.

Good grooming isn't just for the interview, it's for every day. So make a conscious effort to ensure you are properly groomed before you head off to work. It makes an incredible difference.

57 ✦ TOO MUCH PERFUME/COLOGNE

You know the type. They come to work ready to impress. They're well coiffed, nails done, straight pleats, and walking tall. Then they pass you by and *bam,* you're smacked in the face with enough fragrance to make you lose consciousness.

Wearing too much perfume or cologne in the workplace can be a real source of contention. Some people don't feel dressed unless they wear some kind of fragrance. Others may be highly sensitive to perfumes or colognes. Some even suffer asthma attacks, migraine headaches, hives, or other reactions. So it's important to know how much is too much.

A good rule of thumb, especially in an office where you are surrounded by cubicles, is to not wear any perfume or cologne. If you must, use it very sparingly.

It comes down to respect—wearing overpowering perfume or cologne is inconsiderate and disrespectful to your colleagues, something your superiors frown upon.

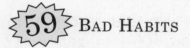

58 — BE CALM AND CONTROLLED

Your demeanor is another important aspect to your appearance. The person who possesses a calm disposition, one that is controlled and confident, is the one whom others go to in times of crisis. They are the people who are trusted to keep a level head when everybody else is in a tizzy.

Are you the calm and controlled type? If not, there are some steps you can take to help you remain calm when life throws you a curve.

First, learn all you can about your job and become so proficient at it that you can practically do it with your eyes closed. The more confident you are in your abilities, the less stressed you are when problems arise. Then, learn what you can about other positions within your organization. This will make your value soar.

Don't forget to breathe. Simple breathing techniques can help you maintain a calm exterior.

59 — BAD HABITS

We need to discuss one more aspect of appearance—bad habits. Bad habits are those annoying things you do that you've been doing much of your life. You do them so much that you usually don't even realize you're doing them.

Some habits are more noticeable, such as swearing and picking your nose. Others are things we do without thinking, such as when you twirl your hair, fidget, or drum your fingers during a meeting.

Other bad habits to be aware of and break include:

- Procrastination
- Tardiness
- Too much chitchatting with colleagues
- Clipping your nails at your desk
- Loud talking
- Being a busybody

Bad habits in the workplace can cause some real problems when it comes to job security. So you need to make yourself aware of your bad habits and take steps to change.

Summary

I hope you realize by now that the way you appear to others really makes a difference in the way you are perceived. The trick now is to use this information to do a thorough self-evaluation, take notes on how you measure up, and do your best to change.

Granted, replacing your worn and perpetually wrinkled wardrobe may not be financially possible right now. But you can still work on your weight, your grooming, your bad habits, and your demeanor. And don't be afraid to check out thrift stores for great, professional-looking clothes.

First impressions are crucial to your success. Developing a professional look will not only build your self-confidence, but it will also leave your superiors with a great impression, which is important for job security.

5 Soft Skills

Do to others as you would
have them do to you.
—LUKE 6:31

Soft skills are characteristics that complement your professional or technical abilities. Employers are increasingly using soft-skills assessments to evaluate the quality of their workers. For this reason, you need to update and improve the soft skills that enable you to excel at the less technical aspects of your job.

Here's a simple explanation of the difference between hard and soft skills. If you repair computers for a living, you use your knowledge of electronics and technical skills to troubleshoot and repair computers. Those are your hard skills. How you interact with customers, vendors, and colleagues are your soft skills.

The following examples of soft skills will help you in every aspect of your job and place you in good standing with your superiors.

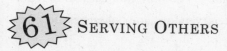

60 SELF-AWARENESS

Self-awareness, often called emotional intelligence, is an important trait in the workplace. The more you know about yourself, your strengths, your weaknesses, your proficiencies, your biases, and so on, the better you are at using or changing them when needed.

When you're self-aware, you are much better at understanding your moods and emotions. This is especially helpful when workplace conflicts arise. When you are aware of what you're feeling and why, you can control your emotions and remain calm.

Another important aspect of self-awareness is understanding yourself well enough to recognize the kind of career you are best suited for. How many of us have spent years moving from job to job, searching for a career that will make us feel fulfilled and happy? An honest self-evaluation, aimed at understanding what you do best, can help you find a career where you will be happy and excel.

61 SERVING OTHERS

In a society where it often seems like it's every man for himself, especially when it comes to business and getting ahead, the person who shows an attitude of service in the workplace stands out. Serving others not only leaves a good impression with people, but it also demonstrates respect, teamwork, and empathy—all highly desired qualities in the workplace.

Serving doesn't mean waiting on someone hand and foot; it can be unpretentious acts of kindness that aid another person. Here are some great examples:

- Holding a door for someone
- Asking a colleague if she would like a coffee refill
- Offering help with a project or difficulty
- Guiding a new employee around the maze of cubicles

Of course, don't let serving others affect your job performance. Simply open your eyes and look around; you'll find ways to serve others in the midst of completing your regular duties.

62 CUSTOMER SERVICE

Customer service is probably the biggest issue for any business. Good customer service keeps customers coming back; bad service sends them elsewhere. Returning happy customers means more money coming into the organization, and that is the bottom line.

Since a lack of good customer-service skills can put your

job at risk, you need to take steps to learn or improve your proficiency in this area. Some of the issues discussed previously in this book are vital for effective customer service, including:

- Empathy
- Integrity
- Communicating clearly
- Verbal communication skills
- Active listening
- Using good manners

Here are a few suggestions to help achieve positive results:

- Never tell a customer, "I don't know." Tell him, "I'll find out."
- Take ownership of a problem, assuring the customer that you will personally follow through.
- Reassure often, tell the truth, and always remain positive.

 TEAMWORK

Whether you work in construction, in a bank, or on the line at a factory, most jobs involve working as part of a team. Your value as an employee is often tied to how well you work with the other members of your team. So teamwork is a skill well worth investing in.

The ability to work together with a group of people can be hampered by other members of the team. The trick is to use your communications skills to help bring the team to its full potential. Even if you are not the team leader, communicating effectively with all members of the team can help bring clarity and mutual understanding.

If you are a team leader, here are some suggestions for building a better team:

- Assess everyone's talents and use them.
- Communicate clear expectations.
- Encourage innovation and creativity.
- Establish respect for all.

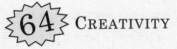 ## 64 CREATIVITY

All of us have the ability to be creative. Sure, some people are gifted with hypercreativity, but we all have skills. The trick is being bold enough to bring your creative side to the surface. This will not only help stir innovation, but it will demonstrate your value to the company you serve.

Many people think of creative people as working in advertising or entertainment. But helping an organization think of new and innovative ways to conduct business also takes a fair amount of creativity.

Simply put, creativity is the ability to rise above conventional ideas, rules, patterns, and such to create significant new ideas, methods, or interpretations. Here are a few simple ways to inspire creative thought:

- Ask, "What if...?"
- Keep an open mind to the ideas of co-workers.
- Look for several different solutions to a problem.
- Seek input/information from diverse sources.
- Don't fear failure.

65 CHARACTER

Yes, character still counts in today's business world. And with dishonest deals, unscrupulous business practices, and corporate thievery running rampant in our society, a person of character is a valuable asset.

Character can be defined as the way you act when nobody is looking. It involves traits such as integrity, honesty, trustworthiness, and kindness. You want to build a reputation in the workplace as someone with all these qualities and more.

But building character takes time. When you try to circumvent the process, you inevitably fail. If you want to start building a reputation for character,

- don't steal time by arriving late, leaving early, and taking extended breaks;

- don't gossip, plagiarize, or cheat on mileage or expense reports;
- be honest in all business dealings;
- avoid "borrowing" tools or other materials from work;
- be responsible;
- give credit where credit is due.

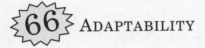 ## ADAPTABILITY

In today's ever-changing work environment, you either adapt or get out of the way. The ability to quickly assimilate new methods, procedures, and technologies is not only key to your success, but it puts you in a much better position when tough staffing decisions need to be made.

Many people resist change. It gets us out of our comfort zone, which causes stress, anxiety, and downright fear—but that can be a good thing. Sometimes a bit of good healthy fear gets us motivated. It also seems to kick in an extra burst of creativity, which is a fundamental component of adaptability.

Change is going to happen, whether you like it or not. Alexander Hamilton once said, "We must make the best of those ills which cannot be avoided." So embrace change and adapt. The more refined your adaptation skills, the higher your worth as an employee.

$\lessgtr 67 \gtrless$ Critical Thinking

Simply put, critical thinking is the mental process we use to conceptualize, apply, analyze, and evaluate information to arrive at an answer or conclusion. The better your critical-thinking skills, the more adept you are at solving problems. Practicing critical thinking also gives you the ability to come up with innovative ways of doing your job, making you a true asset to your employer.

Critical thinking entails thinking independently and developing intellectual strength of mind. It's being able to look at a dilemma from different angles, intellectual perspectives, and beliefs to arrive at an answer that is both logical and workable.

To help you develop better critical-thinking abilities, use the following practices on each issue you tackle:

- Examine and evaluate all assumptions.
- Take note of significant similarities and differences.
- Evaluate the facts and evidence available.
- Distinguish relevant from irrelevant facts.
- Do your research.

$\lessgtr 68 \gtrless$ Problem Solving

One of the more valuable soft skills to have in your arsenal is that of problem solving. A person who can quickly and effectively solve problems gains the trust and appreciation of supe-riors and colleagues alike. An appreciated employee is a more secure one.

We all solve problems every day. But a person with pro-found problem-solving skills knows how to use all of her talents, creativity, technical skills, critical-thinking capacity, and experi-ence to develop solutions that are both innovative and effective.

Brainstorming with a team is a great way to build problem-solving skills and to help develop successful solutions. Brain-storming helps you learn how to attack problems from different angles. It opens your eyes to solutions you may never have thought of. It also helps build teamwork.

You can take the lessons you learn from team brainstorm-ing and apply them to individual problem solving, making you a more effective solver of problems.

 # 69 INITIATIVE

On nearly every employee-evaluation form in business today, one question is universal: "Does this employee exhibit initia-tive?" The answer to that question is crucial to your worth as an employee and to your job security.

Basically, initiative is an aggressive eagerness to do some-thing. Think about your job. Do you have an aggressive ea-gerness to do it? If not, it probably shows. So it's important that we show initiative toward the job we are doing and the company we work for.

Initiative also involves taking the lead to get something done. How many times have you seen something that needed to be done and jumped in and done it, even if it's not your job? That takes initiative. Anticipating a need and fulfilling it is also using initiative.

If things are slow in your area, ask your boss how you can help in another—that also demonstrates your initiative.

70 INFLUENCE

More than likely you do not work in a job that keeps you completely isolated from others. That means that every day you interact with any number of people. Consciously or not, you are influencing them for good or bad.

Especially if you are a senior member of your team, your work ethic, the way you conduct yourself, how you deal with customers, how you communicate, it all has an influence on the people with whom you work. With that in mind, you need to evaluate how you can best use your influence to improve your workplace.

Influence in the workplace is one of those skills that can easily be misused or exploited, so you need to use it wisely. Don't be heavy handed in trying to persuade someone; that only causes fear and anger. Instead, use effective communication skills to gently sway opinions.

The more effectively you use your influence, the greater your value.

71. LEADERSHIP

Exhibiting leadership is more than just the ability to manage people. True leadership can be exercised by anyone within an organization, from the CEO to the person who sweeps the floor. The ability to lead is a trait that will put you in good standing with your superiors.

Leadership is more than telling people what to do and how to do it. It's showing the way. It's demonstrating what to do and how to do it. Leadership takes creativity, innovation, productivity, motivation, and commitment. Effective leaders always lead by example.

How can you demonstrate leadership on your job?

- When a call goes out for volunteers, be the first to respond.
- If you see a new employee doing a task incorrectly, offer to guide him through the correct process.
- Take the initiative when problems arise.
- Be an encourager, a motivator, and a supporter of fellow employees.

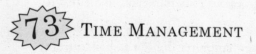

72 ORGANIZATION AND PROFIT AWARENESS

How much do you know about the company you work for? What is its history? How did it start? How do the president and CEO define success? What are your company's financial goals? Do you know the answers to these questions? If not, find out.

The more you know about the company you work for the better. Nothing warms the heart of your superiors more than an employee who truly cares about the company, its goals, its mission, and its bottom line.

Your job now is to research your company and learn all you can about what makes it tick. Then find ways to help the company save and make money. Part of that is to adopt the attitude that you paid for all the equipment within your workplace—tools, computers, paper clips, paper, pens, all of it. Why? Because you take better care of things you own.

73 TIME MANAGEMENT

Time management is one of those things you regularly hear about in training courses on office efficiency. Why? Because efficiently organizing and managing our time is one of the most important things we can do to help ourselves be more productive.

The employee with first-class time-management skills is one who goes to the bottom of any staff-reduction list. That's why you need to take the time to improve the way you manage your time. These suggestions should help:

- *Get organized.* Straighten up your work area; it makes life easier.
- *Organize your priorities.* Make a list of what you need to accomplish, from most urgent to the least.
- *Learn to say no.* If you're overloaded, don't be afraid to say so.
- *Stop procrastinating.* Set manageable goals and reach them…today.
- *Take scheduled breaks and get enough sleep.* Fatigue is a real time killer.

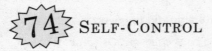 SELF-CONTROL

Perhaps you've worked with someone who would regularly fly off the handle. What can you do? You can hide, look the other way, stare in disbelief, or thank God that you are not the object of this person's wrath. It's not a pleasant situation, and it makes everyone very uncomfortable.

That's why self-control is so important in the workplace. The ability to control your anger or frustration when everything around you is going haywire is a worthwhile trait. Self-control will not only help you to remain calm during the storm, but it will help you to be a more professional and productive employee.

Self-control is also important in other areas. Have you been tempted to take several slices of pizza when the boss is buying? Do you laugh and talk loudly? These can be very annoying too. Control yourself in these situations, and people will think better of you.

75 TEACHING OTHERS

Have you ever started a new job and been totally confused? Even after training? This happens frequently in most every industry. So being willing to take the initiative to help teach a new employee the ropes is an admirable and noteworthy quality.

Taking the time to teach your colleagues is something we don't often think about during the course of our day. We get so busy doing our own thing, trying to reach our own goals, that we miss opportunities to help a fellow employee learn the skills and tricks that will make her, and the department, more efficient.

So don't miss out on an opportunity to teach a colleague. Even if it's not your job, even if the person "should know this stuff already," take the lead and teach. You'll probably make a new friend while you're at it. We can all use more of those!

SUMMARY

Soft skills are an essential part of what makes us well-rounded, effective employees. Without them, we're just robots doing a job. The more highly honed your soft skills are, the better your chances are of landing and keeping a job.

Are you expected to be proficient at all of these skills? No. But if you're lacking in any, adding a few to your repertoire will enhance your value as an employee.

We only skimmed the surface on each of these topics. If you're interested in learning more about these soft skills, look online or go to your local library where you will find resources that will help you reach your goal of becoming a better employee.

6 Improving Presentation Skills

A wise person gets known for insight;
gracious words add to one's reputation.
—PROVERBS 16:21

Improving your presentation skills may not be at the top of your list when it comes to building job security, but this is an area that, while often overlooked, can pay big dividends.

Mastering these skills will give you more confidence, make you look more self-assured and professional, and give your superiors a newfound respect for you. With practice, you will no longer dread job interviews, business presentations, sales demonstrations, or delivering speeches.

The key is to think of giving a presentation as an actor preparing to perform a play. Every actor needs particular skills to give a believable performance. What are you doing when you are delivering a presentation? You're performing. Raising a toast at a wedding or delivering sales presentations—you're performing.

$\lessgtr76\gtrless$ Use Props

One thing every good actor does is use props effectively. Whether it's holding a piece of paper or a pistol, props are used for emphasis and to bring the lines to life. Delivering an effective presentation requires nothing less. What makes an effective prop? Pick items that directly relate to the information you are presenting. If you're speaking about the proper way to hammer a nail, take out your hammer and use it. If you're talking about reducing body fat, wrap up a bag of flour, put it in a bag, and label it "fat." That'll get a laugh and hit home.

Fill your presentation with examples from everyday life. Gather items that complement your examples and bring them out at the appropriate time. Now, don't go overboard and do your best Carrot Top imitation! Use props to enhance your presentation, not to cover up bad material.

$\lessgtr77\gtrless$ Be Animated

Have you ever been to a presentation where the speaker spent the whole time behind a lectern? What the person is saying may be very interesting, but after a while, you're bored out of your mind. Why is that? Because it's static; there's no motion to engage your eye.

What makes a speaker more appealing? Movement. The animated speaker, the one who moves about the stage, who draws your attention, now that is much more interesting.

You need to move around when you give a presentation. Move your arms, gesture, walk around the platform—no matter how small it is. If you need your notes while you speak, carry them with you. Just get away from behind the lectern.

Being animated draws people into your presentation. Your audience pays closer attention. Best of all, they remember more of what you are saying, which is why you're giving the presentation in the first place.

78 ⟩ USE GESTURES

Appropriate, natural gestures help a presenter engage and hold the audience's attention.

Gestures help you emphasize certain key thoughts and drive home points. Even if your audience is just one person, gesturing will draw him in to what you are saying.

Now when we talk of gesturing, hand motions are usually the first things that come to mind. You can point, wave your hands, clench your fist, raise your hand, any number of things to make your point.

Facial expressions are a great way to gesture too. An eye

roll speaks volumes. You can also use your arms, head, legs, even your whole body to make effective gestures. So use gestures, but above all, don't overdo it. You do not want to be remembered as "that guy who jumped around like a kangaroo"— unless you are mimicking zoo animals for a first-graders' class!

79 WATCH YOUR TONE OF VOICE

Have you ever been to a meeting or presentation where the voice of the person speaking made you wish you were any place else? The way a person speaks can make the difference between a good presentation and one that falls flat. That's why you need to be aware of the tonal quality of your voice.

Many times when a person who is uncomfortable speaking in front of people needs to give a presentation, nervousness tends to make her voice rise to a higher pitch. This can be very difficult to listen to, making the presentation less effective. By taking a moment to relax, the voice can come down to a more enjoyable tone.

If you are not sure what your voice sounds like, do your presentation privately for a friend and get some feedback. And until you are more comfortable, ask for a similar critique from a person in attendance at your presentation.

80 ~ ARTICULATION AND DICTION

Articulation and diction are important no matter who you're talking with, at work or in your home. That's why you need to work on your diction and how you pronounce your words.

When some people talk, they tend to mumble. They don't open their mouths; they speak through their teeth; they simply don't speak clearly. When people can't understand what you are saying, your message gets lost.

Here's an easy exercise to help you with your diction and articulation. As you practice your presentation, read your entire speech with a pencil clenched between your teeth, making sure to speak slowly and clearly so that every word is understood. Then do it again without the pencil. You'll find it much easier to enunciate well. The more you practice with the pencil, the better your diction becomes. Then, when it's time to deliver your speech, you will do it wonderfully!

81 ~ CHANGE VOICE VOLUME

What good is a presentation if the audience can't hear it? For some, speaking softly is just part of their personality. But when you speak quietly, it gives the impression that you are insecure in what you are saying. While speaking in front of any group, you want them to believe what you are saying. For that, you need to show confidence, and talking softly won't do that. So you need to speak up.

In acting, speaking loud enough for the audience to hear is called *projection*. Stage actors in particular need good projection skills, and so do you. You can find training online that will help you improve your vocal volume.

But changing your voice volume is also important during a presentation. You can get louder or softer depending on what is being said. Changing the volume of your voice is another way to get people to pay attention.

82 — POSTURE AND BODY CONTROL

How you carry yourself makes a difference in the way you and your message are received. If you give a presentation and you're slouching, fidgeting, and swaying about, people are going to be distracted by your unusual body movements and miss parts of what you are saying.

You want people to remember your message, not your mannerisms; that's why being aware of what your body is doing is so important.

When people get nervous, they tend to exhibit little habits that can be very distracting. They play with their hair, kick their leg, tap their fingers—any number of fidgety manner-isms. The trick is to control fidgeting and avoid distractions.

Your posture is also very important. When you stand tall, you exhibit an air of confidence. The next time you prepare for a presentation, have someone watch you and point out poor posture and mannerisms. It really helps.

83 Look at Your Audience

People who stand behind a lectern and stare at their notes are not connecting with their audience. When you are discussing a project with a colleague at work, if you are not looking him in the eye, the two of you are not connecting completely.

When you do a presentation of any kind, it is crucial that you connect with your audience. If you do, you can be much more confident that your message is being received. Looking at the people in your audience is one of the best ways to achieve that connection.

If you are speaking in a room with several people, di-vide the room into sections. As you speak, take time to make eye contact with someone in each section, periodically changing sections and people. This will entail having a pretty good grasp of your material so you don't have to rely on your notes.

84 Abide by Time Frames

When you give a presentation, if you want to earn the respect and admiration of your peers, start when you say you're going to start and end on time. Keeping within the time limits you have for a particular task or presentation not only exhibits respect for your audience, it also demonstrates good organizational and time-management skills.

When you give a presentation, you're in the spotlight. Everyone is watching you. That's why staying within the time frames set for your address is so important. You want to put your best foot forward and show people your valuable qualities. Starting and ending on time shows that you are well organized, that you know how to get a job done on time, and that you are considerate of your colleagues.

So make sure to practice your presentation with a timer. Make the hard edits to ensure you end on time, even early.

85 Ignore Distractions

All right, this is often easier said than done. Ignoring distractions during a presentation can be quite difficult. But the ability to stay focused and communicate your message, despite what is going on around you, demonstrates your tenacity and strength of mind, two very valuable traits in an employee.

Distractions can be as simple as someone coughing repeatedly or a blaring ambulance siren outside. Others can be more annoying, such as a person arriving late or a cell phone ringing. The ability to press on through these distractions will keep your audience more focused on you and on what you're saying.

Granted, you may be faced with some distractions that you cannot ignore. If you're in a small conference room and someone falls out of his chair, you probably want to pause until he gets back up and settles in. In those cases, respond with grace, and when appropriate, humor.

86 CONNECT WITH YOUR AUDIENCE'S EMOTIONS

One thing that makes a good play or singing performance is the performer's ability to connect with the audience's emotions. It's what causes people to cry during a moving scene or get angry when some calamity befalls the hero. The audience is moved because the material strikes an emotional chord. Your presentations should do the same.

No, I'm not saying you need to make an office manager or colleague weep, but you do want them to feel something. When you can get your audience emotionally involved in what you are saying, your message becomes more powerful and memorable.

So, as you prepare your presentation, take the time to think of ways you can put emotional triggers into your material. Pick an event that occurred at work or in the news or even at home. As your audience relates emotionally to the event, it will bring an immediate connection to what you are saying.

87 KNOW YOUR MATERIAL

If there is one thing that will help you to concentrate on all the other suggestions in this chapter, it is having your presentation memorized. Knowing your material backward and forward, inside and out, will give you the confidence to use your gestures, look at your audience, avoid fidgeting, and ignore distractions.

The better you know your material—the speech, the visuals, the overall topic—the better you can connect with your audience. You will be able to move about the platform or meeting room with confidence, drawing people in to what you are saying and thereby communicating better.

Memorization can be difficult for some. Here are a few suggestions that should help:

- *Use repetition.* Say your speech several times out loud.
- *Small chunks.* Concentrate on memorizing small chunks at a time.
- *Practice makes perfect.* Practice over and over again, using a video camera if possible.

SUMMARY

All of us make presentations of some kind at some time in our career. The more professional it is, the better you look to your superiors. A memorable presentation demonstrates that you know what you are doing, that you are confident, skilled, and prepared. These traits are all highly desired by those who control your job security.

Mastering your presentation skills will not only help you on the job, it can also pay dividends in your regular life. Giving an effective presentation is all about communicating your message so that it is remembered.

Whether you're at a PTA meeting, talking to students during career day at your child's school, or leading a small group at your church, good presentation skills will help your message get through.

7 Thoughts and Actions to Avoid

People ruin their lives by their own stupidity, so
why does GOD always get blamed?
—PROVERBS 19:3

Throughout the course of this book, you've learned about many things you can do to make yourself a better, more valuable employee. While they won't guarantee your job security, they will make you a much more valuable member of your organization. Now let's delve into some specific things to avoid.

Some of what you will read here are actions or thoughts that can hold you back from being the best employee possible. Others can get you in big trouble. If you see your attitudes or actions in any of the subjects covered, then it's time to make a change.

If you are aware of what you may be doing to put yourself in jeopardy when layoffs are imminent, changing those self-destructive thoughts or behaviors will be easier.

{88} TECHNOLOGY ABUSE

You're sitting in front of your computer and getting bored with the report you're working on. So you take some time to check your personal e-mail, where you find that someone wrote a comment on your Facebook Wall, which you naturally respond to. Then you send a "quick" text message after you check your voice mail. This all sounds like pretty innocent stuff, right?

Actually, you are engaging in one of the most common and insidious forms of thievery in the workplace today—stealing time through technology abuse.

While it may seem like many people in your office do the same thing, it's still taking time away from what your boss is paying you to do. Realize it or not, it's also one of the things your boss can surreptitiously track.

Imagine if you were the only person who didn't abuse technology. Your value skyrockets and your job is more secure!

{89} SELF-DEFEATING THOUGHTS

Many people who change jobs or careers several times do so, not because they aren't competent workers, but because they are so filled with self-defeating thoughts that they convince themselves, and others, that they can't do their job.

Self-defeating thoughts include statements like these:

- I can't do it.
- I'm just going to mess this up.
- I'm going to be stuck doing this for the rest of my life.
- Things will never change.

The fact is, when you engage in this kind of thinking, you often do things to make them come true. So the next time you start having negative thoughts,

- tell yourself encouraging statements you would say to a friend who was thinking negatively;
- recognize your self-defeating thoughts and make a case for why the opposite is true;
- build a team of trusted friends who you can contact when negative thoughts invade your brain.

90 ABRASIVE BEHAVIOR

Have you ever worked with someone who had an abrasive personality? If so, you know how stressful it can be. Abrasive coworkers are the ones who tend to be forceful, sarcastic, arrogant, and confrontational. They are very hard to get along with. These are the people with an extreme need for success and perfection.

But abrasive behavior can also include rude or crass behavior. Many a work environment includes a person who tells tasteless or foul jokes, feels the need to curse incessantly, or shares their belching prowess. These kinds of behavior can also make the workplace unpleasant.

For many, abrasive conduct is a cover for insecurity and low self-worth. If you are the person exhibiting harsh or rude behavior, you need to figure out why you act this way and take steps to change.

Like fingernails on a chalkboard, abrasive actions rub people the wrong way, including your superiors.

91 〉 TEMPER, TEMPER

Anger in the workplace is going to happen. But while anger is a common emotion, it is vital to your job security that you keep your temper in check.

Depending on the stress level of your job, you may have to deal with little bouts of anger or huge blowups. The higher the stress, the more frustration and anger set in. But a person's anger may not stem from anything going on at work. It could be a carryover from home or some other situation.

If you are at work and find that your temper is beginning to get the better of you, try these simple suggestions:

- Remove yourself from the situation.
- Talk with someone outside of work who can help give you a different perspective.
- Get away, take some deep breaths, and do some relaxation exercises, which you can find online.

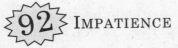 IMPATIENCE

Impatience is another easily recognizable trait. You're waiting to use the copier, and someone has a very long document. You stand there and sigh heavily. You tap your foot, look at your watch, and search in vain for another copier to use. The more you wait, the more your frustration and anger grow.

If others can sense your frustration and impatience, it makes them feel very uncomfortable. Your boss knows when you are constantly annoying people through your impatience. That's why you need to take steps to curb your impatient mannerisms and chill out.

Here are some tips to help you manage your impatience:

- Give yourself plenty of time.
- Expect problems or delays—things don't always go as planned.

- Find something to occupy your mind—think of ways to distract yourself from waiting.
- Accept the fact that you can't control everything.

93 BLACK-AND-WHITE THINKING

Black-and-white thinking severely hampers your ability to excel at your job. It's the kind of philosophy that causes you to be closed-minded, narrow in your thinking, and uncreative. Will that improve your job security? No. Innovation, out-of-the-box thinking, and the ability to inspire creative thinking will.

Black-and-white thinking tends to be pessimistic and self-defeating. Most black-and-white thinkers live in a world of extremes. They use words like *always* and *never*. Life is either great or horrible; you're either smart or stupid; people either love them or hate them; there are no gray areas.

The problem with black-and-white thinking is that it restricts creative thought. Creative thinking is what allows a person to be an effective problem solver, an excellent critical thinker, innovative, flexible, and empathetic—all traits your employer is looking for.

So allow some gray into your thought process and see how far it takes you.

 94 GOSSIP

For many of us, listening to gossip is like free pizza in the lunchroom—it's hard to resist. It's something that occurs in just about every office in probably every industry. But just because gossip is prevalent, that doesn't mean it isn't wrong or that your boss isn't noticing that you engage in it.

Gossip is an insidious destroyer of morale in the workplace. It causes hurt feelings, resentment, anger, and a loss of productivity. The more you engage in gossip, the more your job is in jeopardy, because employers are beginning to crack down on it more and more.

So what can you do?

- Don't participate in gossip. Don't pass it or listen to it.
- Ask yourself, "How would I feel if someone said something like this about me?"
- Act as if everything you say is broadcast across the airwaves for everyone to hear.

95 "I'M INDISPENSABLE"

In today's economy, you will find a huge contingent of people standing in unemployment lines who, before they received their pink slip, thought, "I'm indispensable." The minute you fool yourself into thinking that you are indispensable is the very moment when you begin to get complacent.

Perhaps you've been at your job for several years. You know the company inside and out. There are things you can do that nobody else can. But because you feel indispensable, you begin to lose your edge. You come in late a couple of times, you miss a meeting, and you're not as innovative as you used to be.

The fact of the matter is that nobody is indispensable. From the CEO to the floor sweeper, if any of these people left, the company *would* find a replacement, guaranteed. So you need to do whatever it takes to fight complacency and maintain your competitive edge.

96 "LONGEVITY MEANS SECURITY"

I worked for an organization that has been in business for over thirty years. There were people who had been with the company almost from its inception. When the economy necessitated a reduction in force, several twenty-year-plus employees were laid off.

Just because you've been with a company for several years is no guarantee that your position is secure. Why?

- Employees with seniority usually earn higher salaries.

- A person's education may be outdated.
- As technology changes, new skills are required.

When a business is looking for ways to save money, a person with a high salary makes an easy target, especially if the company can find a younger employee who will do the job for much less. Not much you can do about that.

You *can* update your skills and learn new technologies. You will not only increase your value as an employee, you're more employable if you're laid off.

97 "My Education Brings Security"

How much education do you have? Do you have an undergraduate or graduate degree? If so, that's great! But it's no guarantee that your job is secure. Even someone with an MBA, who thinks that her degree alone will keep her safe, is delusional.

No amount of education can help you if you are not a good employee. You may be intelligent and smart as a whip, but if you lack skills that are vital to your company's changing technological needs, your value degrades.

So you need to be constantly looking for ways to update and learn skills that will enhance the degree you already have. There have been innovations in nearly every industry. Even if your employer isn't using them, chances are they will in the near future. If you already know your way around this new technology and can use it with ease, your value greatly increases.

98 JUST ENOUGH TO GET BY

If there is one thing that will cause your boss to select you—instead of a co-worker—as the one to let go during a layoff, it's your decision to do just enough to get by.

Employers aren't looking for employees who do an adequate job. They want people who are go-getters—people with initiative who will do whatever it takes to get the job done. But many employees adopt the attitude that they are doing their job, they get things done eventually, and the boss should be happy. *Wrong!*

What is your attitude toward your job?

- Do you arrive and leave in accordance with your set schedule?
- Do you accept overtime?
- Do you volunteer to take on new projects?

If you answered no to any of these questions, then it's time for you to take some initiative and show your boss that you are a loyal, tenacious worker.

99 PROCRASTINATION

Procrastination is one of those traits that will keep you from being the best employee you can be. It will also hold you back from being a standout employee in the eyes of your superiors.

Procrastinators say, "Never do today what you can put off until tomorrow." It's not that they can't do the job; they just get this mind-set that makes them put things off. Procrastinators

- think that putting the project off will motivate them;
- get hung up by details;
- are angry that they have to do the job in the first place.

There are any number of reasons why we procrastinate. The trick is to overcome them and get to work. Here are some tips:

- Break projects into small chunks.
- Write down a simple plan of action.
- Decide how much you can do in a set time frame.

SUMMARY

Some of our thoughts and behaviors are deeply ingrained in our personality. Changing them can be difficult and take a very long time. But in today's economic climate, where employers are under considerable pressure to find ways to save money and cut waste, changing the way we think and act is vital to our job security.

It is important for you to do a truthful and thorough self-evaluation to discover the errant thoughts and actions that are holding you back. You may need someone to help you dispose of some of the self-defeating thoughts rolling around in your brain. A trusted friend, counselor, or pastor can help guide you through this process.

And don't let complacency rob you of your passion for your job.

More 99 Ways for
only $5.99!

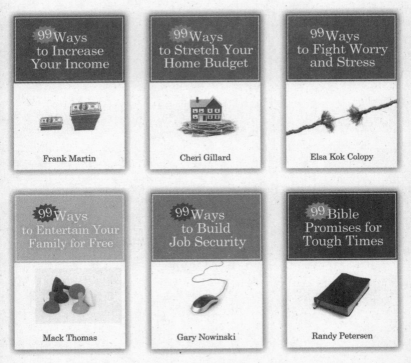

In challenging times we all need advice on how to overcome stress and find encouragement. The 99 Ways books offer up-to-date, practical, and reliable information in a succinct format at a price anyone can afford.

WATERBROOK PRESS
www.waterbrookmultnomah.com